FOOTBALL LEGENDS

Troy Aikman

Terry Bradshaw

Jim Brown

John Elway

Brett Favre

Michael Irvin

Vince Lombardi

John Madden

Dan Marino

Joe Montana

Joe Namath

Walter Payton

Jerry Rice

Barry Sanders

Deion Sanders

Emmitt Smith

Lawrence Taylor

Steve Young

CHELSEA HOUSE PUBLISHERS

FOOTBALL LEGENDS

JOHN MADDEN

Bruce Chadwick

Introduction by
Chuck Noll

CHELSEA HOUSE PUBLISHERS
Philadelphia

Produced by Daniel Bial and Associates
New York, New York

Picture research by Alan Gottlieb
Cover illustration by Bill Vann

First Printing

1 3 5 7 9 8 6 4 2

Library of Congress Cataloging-in-Publication Data

Chadwick, Bruce.
    John Madden/Bruce Chadwick; introduction by Bruce Chadwick.
    p. cm. — (Football legends)
    Includes bibliographical references and index.
    Summary: Traces the football career of the former head coach for the Oakland Raiders
and popular television announcer, John Madden.
    ISBN 0-7910-4399-1 (hardcover)
    1. Madden, John, 1936–   —Juvenile literature. 2. Football coaches—United
States—Biography—Juvenile literature. 3. Sportscasters—United States—Biography—
Juvenile literature. 4. Oakland Raiders (Football team)—History—Juvenile literature.
[1. Madden, John, 1936–   . 2. Football coaches. 3. Sportscasters.] I. Title. II. Series.
GV939.M28C53   1997
796.332'092—dc20
[B]   96-34788
                                                                                  CIP
                                                                                   AC

CONTENTS

A WINNING ATTITUDE

Chuck Noll

Don't ever fall into the trap of believing, "I could never do that. And I won't even try—I don't want to embarrass myself." After all, most top athletes had no idea what they could accomplish when they were young. A secret to the success of every star quarterback and sure-handed receiver is that they tried. If they had not tried, if they had not persevered, they would never have discovered how far they could go and how much they could achieve.

You can learn about trying hard and overcoming challenges by being a sports fan. Or you can take part in organized sports at any level, in any capacity. The student messenger at my high school is now president of a university. A reserve ballplayer who got very little playing time in high school now owns a very successful business. Both of them benefited by the lesson of perseverance that sports offers. The main point is that you don't have to be a Hall of Fame athlete to reap the benefits of participating in sports.

In math class, I learned that the whole is equal to the sum of its parts. But that is not always the case when you are dealing with people. Sports has taught me that the whole is either greater than or less than the sum of its parts, depending on how well the parts work together. And how the parts work together depends on how they really understand the concept of teamwork.

Most people believe that teamwork is a fifty-fifty proposition. But true teamwork is seldom, if ever, fifty-fifty. Teamwork is *whatever it takes to get the job done.* There is no time for the measurement of contributions, no time for anything but concentrating on your job.

One year, my Pittsburgh Steelers were playing the Houston

Oilers in the Astrodome late in the season, with the division championship on the line. Our offensive line was hard hit by the flu, our starting quarterback was out with an injury, and we were having difficulty making a first down. There was tremendous pressure on our defense to perform well—and they rose to the occasion. If the players on the defensive unit had been measuring their contribution against the offense's contribution, they would have given up and gone home. Instead, with a "whatever it takes" attitude, they increased their level of concentration and performance, forced turnovers, and got the ball into field goal range for our offense. Thanks to our defense's winning attitude, we came away with a victory.

Believing in doing whatever it takes to get the job done is what separates a successful person from someone who is not as successful. Nobody can give you this winning outlook; you have to develop it. And I know from experience that it can be learned and developed on the playing field.

My favorite people on the football field have always been offensive linemen and defensive backs. I say this because it takes special people to perform well in jobs in which there is little public recognition when they are doing things right but are thrust into the spotlight as soon as they make a mistake. That is exactly what happens to a lineman whose man sacks the quarterback or a defensive back who lets his receiver catch a touchdown pass. They know the importance of being part of a group that believes in teamwork and does not point fingers at one another.

Sports can be a learning situation as much as it can be fun. And that's why I say, "Get involved. Participate."

CHUCK NOLL, the Pittsburgh Steelers head coach from 1969–1991, led his team to four Super Bowl victories — the most by any coach. Widely respected as an innovator on both offense and defense, Noll was inducted into the Pro Football Hall of Fame in 1993.

A SUPER COACH AT THE SUPER BOWL

The 1977 Super Bowl was held at the Rose Bowl in Pasadena, California, and pitted two hungry teams against each other.

The Oakland Raiders had been one of pro football's most consistently strong teams in the 1970s. But despite good records and powerful lineups, they had not been to the Super Bowl since 1967, when they lost to the Green Bay Packers, 33-14. Fans either loved or hated the Raiders, who were known for their silver and black uniforms, fearsome pirate mascot, and their rough and tough style of play. In the 10 years since their last Super Bowl appearance, Oakland had won nine division titles but never could get past the AFC championship game.

The players and their coach, John Madden, were tired of losing big games by January 1977. Madden, in his eighth season as head coach of the Raiders, especially wanted to win the Super

Ted Hendricks (left) and other jubilant Oakland Raiders carry Coach John Madden from the field after winning Super Bowl XI in 1977.

Bowl. He had been criticized by Raider fans and the press for not winning a "big one" for several years. Now, in sunny Southern California, he had a chance to win the biggest one of all.

It would not be easy. Oakland had finished the regular season with a 13–1 record, tops in the AFC. But their Super Bowl rivals, the Minnesota Vikings, sported the NFC's best record, 11–2–1. Moreover, Minnesota was just as hungry as the Raiders. The Vikings had made it to three previous Super Bowls—in 1970, 1974, and 1975—but lost them all.

Madden wanted to win so badly that he took extra precautions. He shielded his players from most of the Super Bowl publicity until the week of the game and ordered them to give away their tickets to the game before they left for Los Angeles instead of at the game site, as was the custom. He tried to eliminate all off-the-field distractions. He had to defend his team, too, from the years of press charges that they played "dirty" football and bullied other teams. "We don't seem to play dirty when we get beat," he noted.

In practice, Madden reminded the players that they had reached the Super Bowl by boldly executing a basic game plan, and they would need to stick with it. There would be no tricks for the big game. He took extra steps to make certain that everything went as it always did during the week before the game. Defensive drills were held on Wednesday, as usual, and offensive drills on Thursday, also as usual. He made the offense practice exactly like it did during the regular season. Madden was so determined to make things the same as they always were that he even had the equipment manager run to a store to buy 36 extra footballs for practice when it started to rain, so that Kenny Stabler, who had been the number-one-rated passer during the season, would throw only dry footballs.

The coach himself went through the week just as he always did. He dressed as always: baggy pants, shirts, no tie, and sneakers that were untied. His hair was uncombed, as usual. He waved his arms in the air at practice as usual. He stopped and talked to just about anybody who wanted to talk to him. He was pretty nervous, but he went through the week like it was any other week.

The final practice was the best the Raiders had all year. Stabler was sharp, completing 199 of 200 throws. The large offensive line, as famous for its size as its players' catlike quickness, was in the best shape ever. The defensive backs were looser than at any time during the year. Madden was so confident he told Raiders' owner Al Davis that they were definitely going to win.

He wanted to take back that promise soon after the game began. The Raiders' day began in gloom, when a field goal attempt by placekicker Errol Mann hit the upright and bounced back. A minute later, Raider punter Ray Guy, one of the best in the league, had a kick blocked, and the Vikings recovered at the Raider 3 yardline. The thousands of Raider fans in the Rose Bowl, many sporting clothes emblazoned with the team's pirate mascot, groaned. Madden, so famous for waving his arms on the sidelines, waved them like airplane propellers in an effort to get his defensive men pumped up. He was so excited that he ran halfway down the sidelines when the kick was blocked. The Oakland fans may have been worried, but the Raiders down on the field were not.

"Now we've got 'em where we want 'em," said linebacker Phil Villapiano in the huddle to encourage his teammates.

On the second play, Villapiano tackled Viking running back Brent McClanahan hard as he tried to crash through the middle of the line. McClanahan fumbled, and the Raiders recovered on the 1 yardline. Over on the sidelines, a jubilant John Madden was jumping straight up and down and, of course, waving his arms in joy.

The Raiders moved down the field quickly. At the 1 yardline, Stabler passed to tight end Dave Casper for a touchdown. A few minutes later, Stabler hit flanker Fred Biletnikoff with a 17-yard pass, and the receiver struggled to the 1 before finally being pulled down to the turf. Pete Banaszak scored on the very next play, and despite a missed point-after kick, Oakland took a 16-0 lead into the lockerroom at the half. Madden told his players that they were winning and playing well, but that they could not let their guard down against the Vikings. The Vikings had staged several great comebacks during the year and could do it again.

He was right. The Vikings never gave up. Minnesota pulled to within 16-7 in the third quarter, when Fran Tarkenton threw an 8-yard touchdown pass to Sammy White. The Vikings were on the move again in the final quarter, when Raider Willie Hall intercepted a Tarkenton pass at the Oakland 30 yardline and returned it to the 46. Madden immediately ordered Stabler to throw deep, and Fred Biletnikoff hauled in a 48-yard toss at the 2. Banaszak scored again to give the Raiders a commanding 26-7 lead.

Time was running out, so the Vikings went to

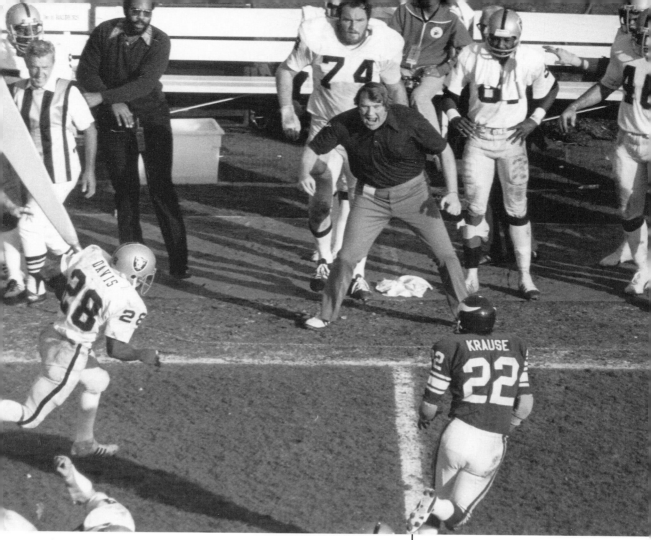

Madden cheers as Clarence Davis earns a first down in Super Bowl XI before Viking safety Paul Krause can force him out of bounds.

the air on almost every play. The team drove further and further down the field. The Raider defense, so loose in practice, was ready for the air attack. With just six minutes left, Raider Willie Brown picked off a Viking pass at the Raider 25 and raced 75 yards for a touchdown as Oakland fans roared. The Raiders were now ahead 32-7. The Vikings scored again, but it didn't matter. Madden and the Raiders would go on to win the Super Bowl, 32-14.

The Raiders played as balanced a game as they had all year. Ken Stabler completed 12 of 19 passes for 180 yards. Fred Biletnikoff caught four passes for 79 yards and Dave Casper four for 70 yards. Running back Clarence Davis rushed for 137 yards.

The star tandem of receiver Fred Biletnikoff (left) and quarterback Ken Stabler celebrate their status as world champions after the Super Bowl.

The Vikings knew they had been defeated by a superior team. "The Raiders just totally dominated us. We were up. We had the emotion, but you have to make the plays to keep it going. They beat us badly," said Tarkenton, one of the sport's legendary quarterbacks.

The defense held the Vikings' offense to 86 yards in the first half. The defenders celebrated wildly in the lockerroom. "They called us a junk yard defense," shouted defensive lineman Otis Sistrunk over the popping champagne corks. "Well, we showed 'em."

Coach John Madden had directed a well-planned attack that saw the Raiders run when Minnesota expected a pass and pass when Minnesota expected a run. He was cautious when he had to be and daring when he had to be. "We didn't want to wheel and deal it," said the coach after the game. "None of that two shots at the line and then pass stuff. We wanted to let it fly."

He paused amid the cheering and then told reporters that "nobody can ever say that we can't win the big one again."

Some of the Raiders in the lockerroom crowd-
ed around Stabler, who shunned the spotlight.
"It was just good execution," he said, refusing
to take credit for the victory.

"He called a super game," insisted lineman Art
Shell. "He was like a computer. He mixed our
passes with the run so well the Vikings could-
n't handle it."

Owner Al Davis understood that most of the
credit should go to Madden. "This establishes
John Madden as a truly great football coach from
an organizational standpoint. It will be only a
matter of time before he is recognized as the
game's greatest coach," he said.

The Super Bowl victory ultimately changed
Madden's life. He was no longer regarded as
someone who could not win the big game. Rather,
he had achieved every coach's great goal. The
game, watched by most sports fans, also made
him a very famous figure. All of these factors
soon made it possible for him to leave the game
when he stood at the top. Only a few years later,
he would take the elevator to the press box and
shine on another stage, as one of television's
best broadcasters.

2
GROWING UP IN FOOTBALL

John Madden was always big. He was the largest boy in his neighborhood in Austin, Minnesota, where he was born in 1936 and lived until he was five years old. His family moved to the suburban town of Daly City, California, in 1941, the year America entered World War II, and John spent the rest of his boyhood there.

Daly City sits snugly on the southern rim of the San Francisco area. John played football there as a kid and later in high school. His best friend was neighbor John Robinson, who also played football and grew up to become the head coach at the University of Southern California and for several pro teams. Madden and Robinson spent most of their free time together. When they weren't on the football field they jumped onto buses and went to San Francisco.

It was a good time to be a boy—and a football player—in the San Francisco area. California did not have a National Football League team, but it had numerous minor league football teams.

Tackle John Madden shows off the Philadelphia Eagle uniform he briefly got to wear as a pro player.

When Madden was 10 years old, he was thrilled to learn that the brand new All-American Football Conference, a rival to the NFL, was siting a new team in San Francisco. Fans in the area finally had their own pro team to cheer on. The new league collapsed in 1950, but some of its teams, including the San Francisco 49ers, Los Angeles Dons, and Cleveland Browns, became teams in an expanded NFL.

Madden and Robinson often went to nearby St. Mary's College to watch the 49ers when they set up training camp just before the season began. During the season, the two friends sneaked into Kezar Stadium in San Francisco to watch games. In those days, pro football was not as popular as it is today, so finding good seats for the game was easy once the boys sneaked past guards.

Madden and his friends in Daly City did not have much money, so for their playground games they bought used sports equipment from local semi-pro teams or wore hand-me-down shoulder pads from older kids. "I don't remember ever playing with a bat that wasn't taped up or nailed together, or with a ball that had a real cover," Madden said.

Madden played well as a lineman for the Jefferson Union High School in Daly City, but he was just as good at baseball. He was the team's catcher and upon graduation was drafted by both the New York Yankees and Boston Red Sox for their minor league systems. He turned them down to stay in football. He went to San Mateo Junior College and then won a football scholarship (along with buddy Robinson) to the University of Oregon. Robinson finished college there, but Madden was hurt during his freshman year and moved on to a number of other colleges. He first transferred to Grays Harbor College, in Washington, and then to the College of San Mateo, near San Francisco, and then won another football scholarship, this time to Cal Poly-San Luis Obispo College.

Madden felt very much at home at Cal Poly. He played tackle on offense and defense and, being curious, peppered coaches about their jobs and learned as much as he could about all aspects of the game. Cal Poly had two good seasons with Madden on its line, compiling an 18-2 record.

"I really enjoyed Cal Poly," said Madden, who earned a degree in education there. "It was a men's college when I got there, and small, probably less than 5,000 students. You didn't even have to comb your hair. You just got up and went to class."

Madden was worried that pro teams might miss him at the tiny California college. He was wrong. The Philadelphia Eagles picked him in the 21st round of the 1959 draft. Madden flew to Philadelphia with great hopes. After all, at 6'4", 277 pounds, he was certainly big enough to play in the NFL. Unfortunately, his pro career did not even last a single summer. Madden injured his knee midway through training camp and knew that his days playing football, which he loved so much, were over.

Madden was uncertain about what he wanted to do, but he loved being around people, particularly kids. So he went back to school, at Cal Poly, to get a master's degree in education so that he could become a teacher. He met his wife, Virginia, there. He stuck to his plan and began to teach at San Luis Obispo High School. In the back of his mind, he wanted to be a football coach. He had spent hours watching game films and talking football with Eagles quarterback Norm Van Brocklin while his knee was mending at the Eagles training camp. He was hooked on the idea of being an NFL coach some day.

He got his first chance to coach when his high school asked him to coach the football team during spring practice. The athletic director, Phil Prijatel, then recommended him to Al Baldock, the coach at Allan Hancock Junior College, in Santa Maria, as an assistant coach. That started Madden's coaching career.

Madden enjoyed one of the most successful coaching careers in football history. He moved up the ladder quickly after he led Hancock to a 13-5 record in his two years there.

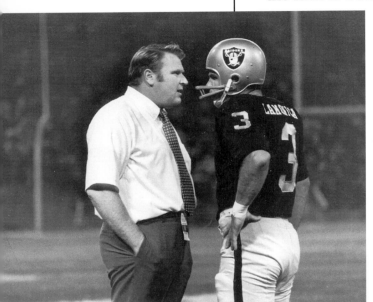

Madden was still a young man when he was named coach of the Oakland Raiders. Here he shares some of his wisdom with quarterback Daryle Lamonica.

Determined to learn all he could about coaching, he went to different coaching clinics and at one met football immortal Vince Lombardi and Don Coryell, head coach at San Diego State University. A year later, Coryell hired Madden as an assistant coach. Madden learned everything about pro football plays at San Diego State because Coryell, later famous as "Air Coryell" for his wide-open passing attacks as coach of the San Diego Chargers, used a pro-style offense.

Madden also became very involved in player recruiting for San Diego State. He would drive from city to city in California and visit nearby states in an effort to interest top high school players to enroll at his college. He recruited well and made solid connections with coaches and fans throughout the state.

John Rauch, the head coach of the Oakland Raiders, was impressed by the performance of San Diego State's team. Oakland was one of the best teams in the American Football League, the other pro league which rivaled the NFL from 1960 to 1970. The Raiders were owned by Al Davis, a man who wanted to make his team the best in the league as soon as possible and, if there was ever a merger, the best in all of pro football. He told Rauch he needed the best assistant coaches to help develop the already successful Raiders into an even better team. Rauch had met Madden several times and was impressed by his football knowledge, coaching skills, and, most of all, his great ability to get along with players. He hired him as linebacker coach.

Madden was an immediate success with the Raiders, who won the AFL championship in 1967 and went to the Super Bowl for the first time that year. Madden impressed the owner, Davis, too, with his likable personality. When Rauch suddenly quit in 1968, Davis asked Madden to step in as the head coach.

Over the years, many people, particularly sportswriters, have criticized Davis for being headstrong and for interfering with his coaches (which is why Rauch left). Davis never appeared that way to Madden. "I found him to be a great owner," Madden said. "In all my years as a head coach, he never turned me down for one thing I wanted. I always wondered how they figure an owner can't interfere. He owns [the team]. How can he not interfere?"

Madden was just 32 years old when he toook over the Raiders in 1969. One of the youngest coaches in NFL history, he inherited a team of "free spirits" from Rauch, men who were certainly not traditional NFL players. They were a wild bunch and did strange things. For example, a coach once caught Dave Casper on the sidelines with his helmet off on a hot day. The coach told Casper to keep his helmet on at all times. So Casper, a bit of a clown, put his helmet on after he showered and wore it to the team lunch, eating through the face guard. Madden, not the coach involved, still laughs about the story.

Another free spirit was big Ben Davidson, who stood 6'8", and weighed 280 pounds. He had the team put a huge photo of him creaming Jets' quarterback Joe Namath on the wall of the executive office. And there was George Buehler, who got ready for a game in which he would have to block 300-pound Louie Kelcher by practicing on the largest object he could find — a Coke machine. Lineman Harry Schuh dieted by consuming whole pizzas by himself. Ken Stabler would sneak out of his room after curfew and try to fool coaches by putting a five-foot-high lamp under his bed sheets to look like his body; on the very first night he tried this ruse, it failed because the coach flipped on the wall light switch and Ken's "body" lit up under the sheets.

As a coach, Madden often shared his opinions loudly with referees.

Otis Sistrunk, whom Madden kept calling "Treetrunk," arrived at the Raiders training camp completely bald. He was so fearsome looking and so odd that broadcaster Alex Karras, when asked what University Sistrunk was from, said, "The University of Mars." Bob Brown, "the Boomer," arrived in 1971 and wanted to show his new teammates how tough he was. He took his helmet off at practice the very first day, slowly walked to the end zone, lined up in a three-point stance, and charged the goal post, knocking it down.

Another favorite character was linebacker Ted Hendricks, whom writers called the "Mad Stork." Hendricks' finest moment was probably the day he saw a little girl riding a horse next to the Raiders' practice field. He talked her into letting him ride the horse right onto the practice field, in his uniform, and then got off and lined up like nothing was strange. Hendricks once complained that he had too much odd competition. "Everywhere else I've played I've been known as colorful. But around here I'm quite boring."

Madden was familiar with NFL offenses, particularly with the new emphasis on passing. He knew he needed an explosive offense and developed one quickly. Stabler and his backup, veteran George Blanda, were two of the best quarterbacks in the NFL and were helped out by great receivers, including Fred Biletnikoff. Everyone who worked with Biletnikoff was amazed by his skills. Steve Tensi, his quarterback at Florida State University, was one of them: "[Biletnikoff] was not fast, yet he always somehow managed to get behind defensive backs who were much faster than him. He also had very soft hands and he could catch any kind of ball you'd throw him.

He would be completely off balance and if a ball hit his hands, he'd hang on to it."

Madden also had a good group of running backs in Mark Van Eeghen, Clarence Davis, Marv Hubbard, and Pete Banaszak.

A tackle in college, Madden was convinced that the key to success was a tough offensive line. He built one with All-Pro players such as Casper, Art Shell, Gene Upshaw, Jim Otto, Henry Lawrence, and Dave Dalby. Casper, Shell, and Otto are already in the Football Hall of Fame; Gene Upshaw later gained renown for serving as head of the football player's union.

The coach, untraditional himself, kept everyone in order but let people have fun. Players appreciated his leniency (he never really enforced team dress codes, for example) and the ease with which they could talk to him. Madden held few formal meetings and preferred to chat with players about their problems wherever he found them, whether on the practice field, the locker-room, or a local restaurant. They responded by playing well for him.

Madden seemed to enjoy the strong personalities of his players. "My guys were different," he admitted, "but they rarely broke the only three rules I ever laid down: be on time, pay attention, and play like hell when I tell you to."

"Over the years, our players would sometimes get into scrapes. John would be there day and night, fighting to help them," said Upshaw.

Biletnikoff liked Madden, too: "He played in college and knew what everything looked like from a player's point of view. He understood players. You could go to him and say, listen, I don't think this will work and he'd listen and often

This photo of Ben Davidson squashing New York Jet quarterback Joe Namath hung in the Raiders' front office.

agree with you and change something. I enjoyed playing for him."

Sportswriters enjoyed Madden's easy sense of humor and his casual style. "Not many football coaches are so free of an ego display as Madden, so outspoken, in common sense terms, so down to earth in player relations," wrote a columnist for the *New York Times*. "He doesn't hide his emotions on the sidelines or in conversation. His lack of pomposity and his low profile approach to his job do not shade over into the kind of walking computer image some other coaches project."

The Raiders went on to become one of the most successful teams in NFL history under Madden. Through all the years, he constantly improved as a coach. His players trusted his instincts as often as they did his playbook.

One of Madden's shrewdest coaching moves involved George Blanda, a placekicker and quarterback. In 1970, Blanda was 42 years old. He could still kick field goals well, but he had not started as a quarterback for many years; few teams would have considered letting him back up the quarterback position. Nevertheless, when starter Daryl Lamonica became injured, which was frequent that season, Madden did not hesitate to utilize the veteran. Blanda responded by having one of the greatest seasons of any player in football history, kicking last-minute field goals and throwing heroic touchdown passes.

John Madden was also a colorful coach. He arrived in an era when most NFL coaches were rather unemotional, even in close games. Madden was a circus of emotions. He would constantly wave his arms, yell as loud as he wanted to, run up and down the sidelines, and howl at the men in the striped shirts.

Madden retired from coaching at the end of his 10th season, satisfied he had accomplished all he had set out to do. He had won 103 regular-season games, more than his idol, Vince Lombardi, did. He reached the 100 mark in his 10th season; only Don Shula had reached it so early. His teams never had a losing season; in fact, they finished first in their division eight times and second twice. His teams were never outscored in a season; in 10 years, the Raiders scored an average of over 34 points a game and allowed an average of under 24 points. To this day, he has the highest winning percentage of any coach with 10 years of NFL experience.

When Madden retired in 1978, he told the press that if he remained on the sidelines he would "burn out" and cease to be effective. His emotional, hard-driving coaching style had led to bleeding ulcers, a serious and painful condition. His time with the Raiders, often on the road, had taken him away from his wife and two sons, Mike and Joe, and that was another reason to quit. He was only 42 when he retired, still a very young man, and he had no plans at all.

After the Raiders crushed the Pittsburgh Steelers, 24-7, in the 1976 AFC championship game, Madden took a dressing room dowsing along with Gene Upshaw (left), and Willie Brown.

3

THE MAN
IN THE BOOTH

"As an analyst at NFL games, the most important thing I do is tell the viewers what I honestly think about what's going on out on the field," said Madden in his book *One Size Doesn't Fit All.*

That sums up his appeal. John Madden was not the first former coach or player to become a broadcaster, nor will he be the last. Many dozens of coaches and players have tried it. Television networks are eager to hire former coaches and players because nobody understands the game like they do. Network executives want these men to explain what is a very complex game in simple terms, make the viewers understand why something happened, predict what might happen next, and, finally, make all of it seem exciting, even in a 44-0 game.

Many former coaches and players can do a decent job as a broadcaster, but few have been

Although Madden was never short of things to say, it took time before he was comfortable announcing a game.

outstanding. It is even harder to be outstanding over a period of years, as the game and players change. John Madden is a rare exception. He has carved out a career spanning more than 15 seasons and has become television's most popular football broadcaster.

One of the reasons why John Madden is so good, and so popular with fans, is that he explains each play quickly, tracing player movements with yellow lines on his beloved telestrater. He talks as a coach, not a journalist, and gives a coach's insight. He is up to date on all the players because he does considerable research on each team during the week.

The real reason, though, is that when you watch him or listen to his voice on television, you firmly believe that he is right there in your living room with you watching and talking about the game, waving his arms, maybe trying to talk with potato chips in his mouth and washing them down too quickly with a soda.

Roger Cohen, chairman of the Rutgers University journalism department, who has studied Madden's style for years, thinks fans identify easily with Madden. "Many viewers see television people, whether they're newsmen, sports people or actors, as distant, far-off characters, living different lives than theirs. Not Madden. People see him as one of them, as a sort of 'good ole Uncle Joe' type, the friendly type. They see him as a big teddy bear guy, a guy they would like to have as a buddy," he said.

Sandy Grossman, who has worked with Madden as his television director at all of his games, thinks that Madden learned long ago that his natural personality was a plus as a television broadcaster: "As a coach, he quickly learned

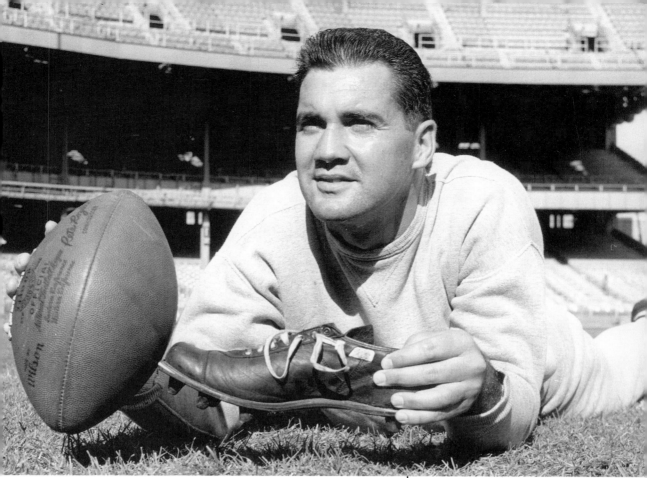

what plays worked and what plays did not. It's the same thing in television. He quickly realized that broadcasting a certain way made him popular, so he stuck with that."

Madden never wanted to be a football analyst on television. He wanted simply to retire, hang out around the house, and spend time with his family. When he left the Raiders, though, his wife was running her own business and his two sons were teenagers. They were all in the middle of their own lives, and the house Madden retired to was very quiet. He was bored.

That same year, Barry Franks, head of a talent agency, asked him if he was interested in doing a screen test for a job as a part-time foot-

Madden's announcing sidekick, Pat Summerall, was a placekicking specialist for the Chicago Cardinals and New York Giants from 1952 to 1961.

ball analyst for CBS. Madden was not. Franks then told him that a production company was putting together a new comedy series called "Cheers." They were interested in using Madden to play the character of a former football coach on the show. Madden turned that down, too.

Franks asked him about the football analyst job again a few weeks later. This time Madden, very tired of staying at home, said yes, but only if it was part time. CBS assured him it was. The test went well, and Madden got the job. He had no idea if he would like it or if he would be any good at it because he was so different in his approach to life than just about everybody else.

That first season, in 1979, Madden was paired with former New York Giants field-goal kicker Pat Summerall and a few other announcers. Pat would become his longtime sidekick. Pat would do the play by play, and John would do the color commentary. Madden found out right away that he liked working with Summerall and truly enjoyed announcing. "I surprised myself. I said, 'This is it — this is what I want to do.'"

Madden was an instant hit with the fans. Ratings for the games he and Summerall broadcast together went up. He won the Touchdown Club of America's Golden Mike Award in his third season and his first Emmy Award in 1982 for "outstanding sports personality analyst." He won eight more Emmies over the years, as well as countless awards from various groups for his work as a broadcaster.

Sports Illustrated writers praised him. "In the tedious clutter of commentary that sports television has become, Madden remains forever fresh," wrote Norman Chad. "His insights are unmatched, his humor is original, his manner is unaffected. Yet, for all his down-to-earth dazzle, he seldom overshadows a game. When the outcome is in doubt, he analyzes; when the game is a rout, he amuses....Watching CBS' top team is the best way to catch football on weekend afternoons."

One of the reasons the people in the media and the fans have enjoyed Madden is the all-new football vocabulary he has made up over the years. Don't look in the dictionary. Many of the words Madden uses are not there.

In his rush to describe games, and unhappy with available dictionary definitions, Madden began to make up words early in his career. "Instead of correcting myself and making sure the grammar is right, I just make up a word," he said.

He makes up a lot of action words that seem to come from the pen of a comic-book writer. He will watch a lineman sack a quarterback and, as the quarterback hits the grass, yell into the microphone: "Boom!" He will watch someone make a hard tackle on a running back and shout into his mike, "Whack!" Another favorite for a hard hit is "Bam!" If he can't get "Bam!" out of his mouth, he'll go with "Pow!" He once wanted to say that the San Francisco 49ers play with great finesse. It came out as "the 49ers get finessy on you." "Finessy" is not a word you'll find in any dictionary.

One Madden favorite is the "sweat test," when he decides who plays the hardest by the amount of sweat the television camera picks up on their face. Another is the ankle tackle. He told viewers very seriously that big strong football players have weak ankles. "They have strong arms, strong legs, and strong hands, but nobody has strong ankles. Nobody," said Madden. That's why, he explained slowly, carefully, simply, that the very best place to tackle a strong runner was at the ankles. Later, as viewers watched the game, with no more instruction from Madden, they saw runner after runner stopped cold by ankle tackles.

The broadcaster also invented little phrases that seemed to just pop out of his mouth as he analyzed games, phrases that fans began to use at home, school, and in the workplace. In explaining the rules about when a receiver is ruled inbounds, Madden spontaneously came up with, "One knee equals two feet." In other words, if a receiver gets one knee down before going out of bounds, that's as good as him putting both feet down—the pass is a completion. Anyone who has studied anatomy will tell you that one knee does not equal two feet, but Madden liked the phrase so well, he used it as the name of one of his books.

Before Madden first went on the air, he broadcasted a "practice game" with Bob Costas. While other announcers actually broadcasted a game, he and Costas "practiced" by watching the same game and taping their "broadcast." Madden had some problems. The show's director kept yelling through his headset "Coach, Coach," meaning that he wanted Madden to comment on 49ers coach Bill Walsh, whose picture was on the screen. Madden kept yelling back, "Yeah? Yeah?" thinking the director was yelling "coach" at him because he had been called "coach" by everybody in America for ten years. Then there was the interview. The network arranged for a for-

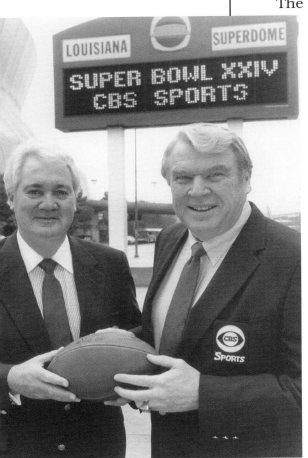

Summerall and Madden have now been play-by-play partners for over 15 years and have covered many of the most exciting games ever played.

mer player to be Madden's halftime guest. The director, on cue, told Madden to start the interview. Madden, who had been interviewed himself thousands of times but had never interviewed anybody onscreen, didn't know what to do.

The network was pleased with the tape, though. Madden just started talking to the former player, and the conversation they had was as good as any interview. By the end of the game, he had started talking about Bill Walsh when the director yelled, "Coach, Coach," into his headset. Madden himself felt very comfortable with the tape. In his book *Hey, Wait A Minute: I Just Wrote a Book*, he said that after that "practice" game he was certain he wanted to be an analyst.

In Madden's first season, CBS paired him with Summerall and others for each game so he could try to adapt to different peoples' styles. The network also put him through a crash course in players' names and numbers to prep him for game-day broadcasts. Over the years, he and Pat Summerall became so familiar with players that they often didn't even need to look at the position/numbers charts sitting in front of them on a table in the broadcast booth. "You get to know automatically where people are on the field. I can tell a guy by the way he moves," said Madden.

Some television experts think Summerall is responsible for much of Madden's success. "If the other broadcaster talked a lot, it would really tone John down," said Cohen. "Pat says very little, just does the play-by-play, and leaves all that time for John to talk. He lets Madden be Madden, and that combination is what is so successful.

4
GAME DAY

Game Day for the football fan begins when the crowd starts its low roar and the kicker gingerly steps towards the ball on its plastic tee and boots it high into the air toward the opposing team's end zone.

For John Madden, game day usually begins some time during the previous week. He learned as a graduate student and high school teacher that preparation is what makes a good teacher. He felt the same way about being a television football analyst. He wanted to be completely prepared before he went into the broadcast booth. He had to know everything about each team and its coach and the important players, if he was going to do his job well.

Madden spends much of the week before a game gathering newspaper clippings about the teams he will see the following Sunday. He watches many football magazine–type shows on tele-

Summerall and Madden go over their game plan before the start of the 1994 NFC championship match.

37

vision. If he can, he watches tapes of the two teams' previous games in the season. He'll watch them the week before if either appears on Monday night football. He will read any public relations information and statistics sheets mailed to him by publicity departments.

He and Summerall, fully prepared from their reading, arrive at the practice sessions of the two teams sometime Friday afternoon or Saturday morning. They spend at least an hour talking to each of the two head coaches to get a sense of where the team is that week — who's hurt, who's in some kind of slump, who's making a comeback. Each coach will go over the season — its highs and lows — and go over a roster list and talk about key players. These sessions, similar to sessions reporters from newspapers also have with coaches, not only allow Madden and Summerall to keep up with injuries, statistics, and team strength, but give them a "feel" for the coach and the team. Anyone in sports will agree that a very upbeat coach and upbeat team, players who are certain they are going to win, will have a psychological advantage over coaches and players who feel "down," who may have lost a few games in a row.

Madden then, on his own, walks around and talks to players. He'll frequently talk to players he knows. He feels it is important to talk to the two starting quarterbacks, the men who run the offense, and some halfbacks and wide receivers. Madden, a former lineman himself, likes to talk to linemen, offensive and defensive. Over the years, his insight about linemen has made his broadcasts much richer than most TV analysts.

Madden often goes over to players he has never met. He tries to pick up information for his broadcast, but most importantly, like any good reporter, he tries to find little stories which can play out for him on game day. He likes to talk to injured players to see if they will be in the game and how they feel. He likes to talk to rookies to see if they are nervous or, if the season is halfway finished, how they are fitting into the team's program. He enjoys discussions with players who are new to a team and veterans who may be taking a team to a playoff. On air, he is an instant encyclopedia of how many times particular players have been in the playoffs for different teams.

Most of all, he likes stories that have some drama in them. He once talked to a field goal kicker, a rookie, who was told by his doctors that his injury would keep him out six weeks. The rookie told Madden he was determined to get back as soon as possible and was kicking not in six weeks but just six days. It made a nice story on game day.

On game day itself, Madden and Summerall arrive early for the game, do some last minute preparations, go through microphone checks and then stand up. Most other broadcasters sit in the broadcast booth. But the former coach and the former field-goal kicker spent their careers standing up and neither likes to sit down on the job. Madden, particularly, enjoys standing up because it gives him a better view of the entire field. Standing, often with arms casually folded across his chest, he talks directly to Summerall as he does his color commentary. He creates a conversational feeling for himself by working that way, and the result is the feeling of conversation for the viewer. The two men almost never watch the game on the television monitor in their booth. They both watch it live, down on the field.

"He can see the entire field, and everybody on it, that way. If he watched a television set he would miss many of the players," said director Sandy Grossman. "It also lets him see the game just as all the fans in the stadium are seeing it and that makes it better for him."

At halftime, Madden and Summerall will go over the results of the first part of the game with each other. They always seem to agree on why teams are playing well or playing poorly. They will go on air when the second half begins with a little analysis of the first part of the game and then tell viewers what the teams will probably do in the second half. They are usually right.

One thing Madden and Summerall never do is go into a broadcast with a definite idea of what the "game story" is going to be. Newspaper reporters often develop a "game story" idea and publish it on the morning of the game. They will write that the game is some kind of a grudge match because one team has not beaten the other in several years. Another "game story" might be a quarterback returning from the injured list, or the first game of a rookie.

Madden stays away from that. He always felt that the "game story" would develop during the game itself. His job is to report the game in

One of Madden's humorous highlights as an announcer: showing the strategy New York Giant linebacker Harry Carson (left) followed before dumping a container of ice water on Coach Bill Parcells.

progress to fans, not to tell them what he or any-one else thought the game would look like. Injuries to quarterbacks in the game then become "game stories," as does the inability of a team to run against another team, or a star quarterback's inability to complete a lot of passes against a particular type of defense. By doing it that way, Madden makes his broadcasts fresh.

Throughout the game, Madden uses the television telestrater, or "chalkboard," to explain to viewers what just happened on a play. His chalkboard quickly became the most popular part of his telecasts.

It came about because of Madden's remarkable ability to see the moves of all 22 players on the field at the same time during a play. He would start talking as the play unfolded and let fans know exactly what was going on. One of the great developments in television in the 1970s, when Madden started in the medium, was instant replay. Later, with the aid of computers and advanced technology, television productions were able to permit the drawing over a screen with a pen or "magic marker." It was suggested to Madden that he used the magic marker to show fans what just happened in a play.

As soon as the play is over and the replay is shown, Madden goes to work. Talking rapidly, but not too rapidly, he watches the frozen screen and circles players. He tells what that player will do by drawing lines showing where he will move. The replay then begins, and the players go exactly where Madden remembered them going on the play. He then analyzes why the play worked or did not work. Sometimes his magic marker lines only show a straight line with a "T" on the end of it for a block. Sometimes they show a half circle tracing the pattern a receiver will follow. Sometimes the lines are very complex, showing the movements of a quarterback, his blockers, his receivers, and defensive backs. It permits viewers, who probably only followed the ball during the actual play, to see how everyone on the field moved and why the play worked and did not work. Only someone with Madden's football experience, and mental quickness, could do it that well.

"Nobody else can do that," argues WFAN's Mike Francesa. "You simply have the ability to watch 22 guys play football at the same time, and explain it in two seconds later, or you don't. Nobody can teach that to you. John is the ONLY man who can do that."

He has become very amusing with his chalkboard. One of the highlights of its use was the day Madden explained carefully to fans exactly how New York Giants linebacker Harry Carson liked to sneak behind the lines of players watching a game near the end, pick up a giant container of Gatorade, and then sneak up behind Coach Bill Parcells and pour it over him to celebrate a big win. He circled Carson as a play began and then explained with his magic marker lines how Carson would move. Sure enough, the player followed the line, picked up the container of Gatorade, and then dumped it over the coach, just as Madden predicted.

Another piece of "Maddenmania" that has creeped onto the pro football landscape is the All-Madden team. Pal John Robinson gave him the idea of a Madden all-star team during the 1985 season. Robinson told Madden he should name a team of unusual players, players the regular all-star teams often overlook. After all, Robinson told his friend, just about everybody else had an all-star team. There were All-Pro teams from the different wire services, all the major newspapers, magazines, and sports groups. There was an annual All-Pro game. Why not an All-Madden team?

The announcer liked the idea and began to work on it. Over the years, it has become a regular part of the football fan's season. The only rule is that all players selected are players John saw during the season. He probably misses some truly great players, or odd players, because he didn't see them live on games he broadcast. For example: Madden and Summerall did not broadcast any Pittsburgh Steelers games in 1995. The Steelers wound up in the Super Bowl and produced several All-Pro players. None were eligible for the All-Madden team, though.

The All-Madden teams usually list the obvious great players but they have included some very strange players. One was the San Francisco 49ers' Jack "Hacksaw" Reynolds, nicknamed because he took a hacksaw and sawed a car in half because of his anger over a loss. Another was Jack Youngblood of the Los Angeles Rams, because in every game he seemed to come off the field with blood on his jersey. The Giants' Phil McConkey was picked because he was a former helicopter pilot and ran onto the field each week waving a white towel over his head. Washington Redskin 305-pound lineman Joe Jacoby was selected because he always had mud on his face. William "The Refrigerator" Perry, who weighs 350 pounds, once caught a pass for the Chica-

William "the Refrigerator" Perry, a 350-pound defensive end who occasionally lined up in the Chicago Bears backfield, was a perennial member of the All-Madden team. Each year, Madden would pick several unusual all-stars for the team.

go Bears, so Madden picked him as a wide receiver. Each year Madden picks at least one player who performs the best "touchdown dance" when he scores.

One year, just for fun, Madden named four quarterbacks to the team — Doug Williams, Wade Wilson, Joe Montana, and Jim McMahon. Another year he picked three centers — Jay Hilgenberg, Billy Bryant, and Jeff Van Note.

Why pick four quarterbacks? Madden followers right away saw his reasoning: What if three got hurt?

There's also a tender side to Madden, and that comes out in his picks, too. He once named wheelchair-bound Mike Utley, who played for Detroit from 1989–91, because he was an example to all Americans of people who fight on despite problems.

That first year of the All-Madden team, CBS-TV producers put through a colorful show with clips of all the players Madden selected. Every year now there is a television show for the All-Madden team. The players even get trophies, special jackets, and sweatshirts for making the team—plus free pizza. It has grown in fame so much that many players who make it display their trophies just as they do for All-Pro teams.

Madden likes the way Detroit Lion runningback Barry Sanders can run even while being grabbed by the face mask.

The team has become a regular part of the season for the television network that works with Madden. Players gladly appear on it to have some fun and poke fun at the broadcaster. The All-Madden team helped make Madden an even better known broadcaster.

Oddly, it was not his years as a football coach or his years in the broadcast booth that made John Madden one of the most famous people in sports — it was a television commercial.

In 1979, the Miller beer company decided to do a series of commercials featuring sports stars talking about its Lite beer. The commercial would feature two sports figures who would argue whether or not the beer tasted great or was less filling. Madden was hired to charge through a wall of paper at the end of the commercials, waving his arms, and yell that he was not the same crazy coach he was in the NFL anymore.

Madden did not look forward to appearing in the ads and even turned Miller down the first time they asked him about the ads. He finally did them — filming them in just a few days — and went home. He forgot about them. They began to run on television a few months later and ran so often on so many channels that they made Madden very famous. People would yell at him at restaurants "tastes great" or "less filling."

Madden had so much fun with people who came up to him to talk about the ads that he decided to do more commercials, for companies such as True Value Hardware and Tinactin.

He was even given his own video football game, "John Madden's Football," produced by the Sega Company, which is revised each year.

5
ON THE ROAD AGAIN

John Madden was never afraid of going head to head with a 300-pound lineman on the field or of colliding with a runner trying to steal home when he played baseball. But he is afraid of flying.

He is not alone. Thousands of people have a fear of flying. Madden always hated planes but, as a player and coach, always had to use them. Looking back, he realized that it was not really a fear of flying but a fear of being confined inside an airplane high up in the sky. He remembered many incidents like that on the ground, particularly when he was a boy, and knew that he suffered from claustrophobia, a common problem for many people. If you feel all pent up, can hardly breathe, and want to scream when you're in a small room or a tunnel or elevator, you have claustrophobia.

As a boy, Madden would never sit in the middle seats of a dining room table but insisted on

The "Madden Cruiser" allows the ex-coach to ride in comfort. Here it takes him through New York City on the way to a game.

sitting near the end. He always liked to keep windows open in any room he was in. He disliked small rooms and loved large rooms. These were all signs of claustrophobia.

He always put up with it because he had to. He was in a business where everybody flew from city to city for games on airplanes. He would have to fly as a television analyst, too, he was told. One day, during his first season as an announcer, he sat down on a plane for a trip from Tampa to San Francisco with a stopover in Houston. Just after the plane took off, he had that dreadful feeling again, only this time it was very bad, so bad that when the plane arrived for the stopover he got off and took a train to San Francisco. He knew he could not fly any longer but also knew that he had to travel great distances to work on television.

The answer, at first, was the train. Madden's work is not like that of most people. The work Madden does during the week — going over statistics and information sheets and looking at game films — he can do at home. He is only required to be somewhere else between Friday night and Sunday night, or during the week for an occasional game. Trains can cover most of the country in just one or two days and can go from California to New York in three.

Madden did not tell people he was using trains at first. People would ask if they could meet him at the airport, and he would laugh and make a joke about not being a king and needing a greeter. He did not want them to know he was arriving at the train station.

He stopped hiding his practice after a few months, and nobody cared. So he began to travel by train all over America. It not only ended his sense of claustrophobia but opened up a whole new lifestyle for him. He got all of his reading and research done on the train and still had plenty of time to watch the country go by outside the windows of the train cars. Madden, one of the friendliest people in sports, also enjoyed all the people he met on trains, people who knew him from television, liked his work, and loved to talk sports. He also found that the rumbling feeling of a train as it races across America made it much easier for him to sleep than anywhere else. He was getting nine to ten hours of sleep and arriving at his destination for a game completely rested, his research done, and in wonderful spirits for the game.

Train travel had one big drawback, though. Trains did not always permit Madden to travel from one city to another on a direct route. He would often have to drive his car eight or nine hours to pick up a train that would take him to Chicago or Miami. It became awkward. By the time he got on the train, he was exhausted from driving 400 miles.

The solution was the "Madden Cruiser," his own customized, 45-foot-long, $600,000 bus. The cruiser, with its own driver (the current regulars are Dave Hahn and Willie Yarborough), is a brand new blue and white bus. Greyhound and Custom Coach, Inc., who customizes buses for many country music and rock stars, renovated it into a traveling home and office for the broadcaster and gave it to him in return for promotional benefits. It has a living room, bedroom, bathroom, kitchen, two stereos, a four-unit intercom, a satellite dish on the roof, an office console with a desk, three telephones, and fax machine. There are two large color television sets, with VCRs attached, so he can watch programs or videos or pop in football game films to study for his upcoming weekend game broadcast. The rooms of the bus were designed by an interior decorator to resemble a typical home.

The need for a bus matched his yearning for traveling across the country at his own speed. He had read John Steinbeck's novel *Travels with Charley*, about a man and his dog who traveled across America, when he was in high school. Somehow, he vowed then, he would do something like that himself.

The Madden Cruiser gives him freedom. He and his drivers map out their trip from one NFL game to another and ride every scenic highway they can find. These trips have taken Madden to cities where he will drop into a restaurant and watch Monday Night Football games with locals, go fishing in the Gulf of Mexico, watch skiers in the Rockies, or visit cities he always read about as a kid. He has developed a list of favorite restaurants in different towns he loves to visit. Madden picks up newspapers in the cities and towns he visits and checks listing for movies that are playing nearby. With no notice at all, the huge Madden Cruiser will pull into a shopping center parking lot and Madden will get out and catch a new movie that he wanted to see, well prepared with candy and popcorn.

His favorite trips are those which take him through rural America. "I enjoy going through small towns," he said. "I sleep a lot during the day and stay up late at night because I like seeing the lights in the farmhouses and wondering what people do. I'll count to the next light and see that the closest neighbor is 20 miles away.

I just make things up and watch tapes and go into the small towns to eat."

The bus quickly became a part of Madden's family. It became part of the American sports fan's family, too. He once interviewed Forrest Gregg, then head coach of the Green Bay Packers, in his stadium office. In the middle of the interview, Gregg, looking out the window, blurted out, "Hey, there's the bus," as if it was a part of Madden himself.

"The bus is not just a way of travel for him, but a way of living. It permits him to ride around the country and meet every kind of person there is," said David Klatell, a broadcast journalism professor at Columbia University. "He finds out what people want in football from these trips. It also lets everybody in America know that he is just an average guy, a very common guy who rides around in a bus. The rich people fly first class or travel in limos. The ordinary people ride the bus. John Madden rides the bus."

New York Giants' quarterback Dave Brown took the first snap of the game, rolled right and tried to force a pass to one of his receivers. Brock Marion, a defensive back for the Dallas Cowboys, moved in front of the Giants receiver and intercepted the ball. Pat Summerall, calling the November 1995 game for FOX-TV, mentioned the names of the athletes as the play unfolded. Even as Marion was celebrating his interception, John Madden started to explain what had taken place and why. "They tried to fool the Cowboys with a bootleg pass," Madden said as the replay showed that Marion was never out of position. "Didn't work," he added, as Marion made his cut and watched the ball all the way into his hands.

John Madden has the rare ability to see what all 22 people are doing on the football field at once. For example, in this 1995 Giants-Cowboys game, he explained who was doing what to whom as Rodney Hampton (left) was stopped by Leon Lett (number 78), who was being blocked by John Elliott.

Madden, high above the field with his FOX-TV broadcasting sidekick, Summerall, shook his head as he looked down at the gridiron. "Emmitt Smith told us yesterday that the Cowboys haven't gotten any breaks. Well, they got one now," said Madden as the Cowboys lined up. He then went on to explain just how Marion made the interception, what it meant to the Giants, and what it meant to the Cowboys.

He barely had time to catch his breath when Giants' defensive back Phillippi Sparks was called for pass interference on the Cowboys' All-Pro receiver Michael Irvin. "Sparks said before the game that he knew Michael Irvin was going to be physical. He said he had to be more physical than Irvin. He looks forward to playing against him," said Madden as he watched the replay. "When Irvin doesn't get one, that's one for Phillippi. He's a scrappy little guy, lots of spirit and life. He has fun out there. He plays football the way it should be played."

Not a moment later, Madden was impressed with the way lineman Larry Allen blocked to spring Emmitt Smith loose for a short gain. Madden immediately moved to his famous "chalkboard," the TV screen on which he can sketch player movements with a yellow magic marker. "See," he said, starting to draw lines that showed how Allen moved forward and then sharply to the right to open a hole for the runner "he does this...."

Madden put down his magic marker. "I've never seen a guy as powerful as Larry Allen," he said.

A few minutes later, between plays, viewers found out that Jay Novacek was injured all week and only practiced on Friday. They learned that Sparks, determined to shut down

Irvin, made up his mind during the week that if Irvin was too physical with him he would try to hold him by grabbing his shirt. He did, was caught, and was given his second penalty. "That's a good technique if you don't get caught," joked Madden.

As the game moved along, it was wonderfully taken over by Madden. He reminded fans that Cowboys' coach Barry Switzer was roundly criticized the week before for trying to get a first down with fourth down and one foot on his own 29 yard line (and failed) and that he, Madden, was completely against it. He turned to Dan Reeves, the often criticized coach of the Giants, and defended him, telling viewers, with the game very close, that Reeves was doing a good job of mixing up his plays. He shrugged his shoulders after his talk on coaches and, as a former coach, told viewers what coaches do about criticism of any kind: "You have to let it go and get on with it. Your last game, win or lose, has to be out of your mind by Wednesday."

He kept viewer attention focused on the continuing battle between Irvin and Sparks. He explained that the key to success for middle linebackers is their ability to tackle runners to prevent big gains. He constantly kept viewers up to date on what Cowboys' star Deion Sanders was doing, whether he's playing offense or defense. (He used the chalkboard to show how the Giants tried to take Deion out of many pass plays by ordering the man he's covering to run across the middle, opening up the sidelines for another pass receiver.) Madden got excited when Brown was sacked, and he quickly told viewers that the key wasn't the man who tackled Brown (Hennings) but the Cowboys' Leon Lett, who charged the quarterback up the middle, pulling two players with him, opening up the lane for Hennings to grab Brown.

Explaining how plays work and don't work is Madden's strength. Like a master auto mechanic, he opens up a car's hood for the viewer and lets them look down at the engine and explains how every part works to make it run. He takes apart plays, step by step and player by player. On a key third-down play in the Dallas - New York game, Giants quarterback Dave Brown was tackled a yard behind the line of scrimmage on a sweep, and Madden zeroed in. "That was a big play for the Cowboys. On third downs, the Giants have been running on Dallas all day. Brown had run on just about each situation. Now, see, the Cowboys have plugged all the lanes Brown could use to get through the line. They did it by having Darren Woodson move up from the corner," he said.

Madden understands that teams often borrow plays from one another. The Cowboys' Kevin Williams caught one pass for a 30-yard gain by running diagonally across the middle of the field. Madden beamed, his voice full of joy. "That's a 49er play!" he said. "Jerry Rice. You go over the middle on a slant so that when you catch the ball you're already in the open field."

Play by play, minute by minute, Madden does what nobody else in television has ever been able to do. He makes the fan watching the game an actual part of the action, putting him inside the heads of all 22 men on the field. He analyzes each play and the moves of the players involved quickly. He second guesses the coaches and the quarterbacks, disagrees with some calls and agrees with others.

He makes strong statements about some players in the game and tries to let fans know how he feels about their future.

"Dave Brown is very effective at looking for soft spots in the defense and either throwing into them or running into them himself....Brown has become a lot more confident, better at play faking...throwing tighter spirals. He is a good young quarterback you can see growing," he said of the Giant quarterback.

Then it was back to the game.

Madden carefully explained how one play collapsed because the Giants' Brown paid too much attention to defensive back Sanders, probably the best in the NFL, and ignored the rest of the field. He explained that a touchdown by Rodney Hampton worked because he ran over the right side of the offensive line, which Madden said was much stronger than the left.

A short time before, Madden left his analysis and went off into a marvelous story about how he bumped into Hampton in the lobby of a hotel the night before. Hampton was there with his high school English teacher, an elderly woman whose strict discipline helped to keep him academically eligible to play football. Hampton had invited her to the game and was introducing her to everyone he knew.

Later, determined to talk about everything the viewer saw on the television screen, Madden went into a detailed analysis of how a player's torn jersey is repaired by punching holes in it

After CBS Sports lost the rights to broadcast NFL football to FOX, Madden and Summerall donned new blazers and continued to educate and entertain their millions of fans.

and sewing it together with shoelaces. From there he moved to an analysis of how sideline telephone headsets worked.

Then it was back to football: an explanation of what truly is the rule on grounding when a quarterback hurls the football into the dirt, why he thinks Sanders is a great back ("If he gets behind you, he's going to go all the way"), why the Cowboys added pass patterns across the field for the first time this season, where the Cowboys are vulnerable, why some quarterbacks are afraid of throwing footballs in the rain.

When the Giants scored a touchdown, he went back to his chalkboard and analyzed it. As always, he used easy terms that everybody could understand. "See, look," he said as Dave Brown started to run to his right and the goal line. "Look at his eyes. He's watching that one player and...there...he knows he can go right...knows that if he can get around that one guy he can score...."

John Madden enjoys his job. Every few months someone asks him if he wants to return to pro football as a coach and he always smiles and says no. The latest "draft Madden" movement started when Don Shula retired as Miami Dolphins coach in 1995. Fans and writers wondered if Madden would do a good job with the Dolphins. Once again, the big man said he was not interested.

"I knew that I was never going to coach again," Madden said. "I never had the passion that I couldn't live without it. I started doing football games on television and for me that took coaching's place."

He feels that those who leave coaching and go back, such as Jimmy Johnson and Bill Parcells, are different. "They can't live without it," said Madden.

Now in his second decade in the broadcast booth, Madden is enjoying himself. He always had fun as a football analyst but now loosens up even more. Recently, after numerous jokes about the Blockbuster blimp, which helps televise the FOX games, Madden challenged the blimp to a race against his bus. His television producer thought it was such a good idea that FOX-TV staged the race from Dallas, Texas, to Shreveport, Louisiana, as an attraction aired as part of its "All-Madden Team" show. (Madden and his bus won the race by 12½ minutes.)

Perhaps the highest compliment paid to Madden was that of numerous television and sports columnists in 1994, when FOX bought the rights to televise NFL games for $1.5 billion. At the press conference to announce the deal, the columnists' main concern was not how much money FOX paid the NFL, not how many games a year would be televised or what FOX was hoping the football coverage would do to help them as a network. The columnists all wanted to know if FOX planned to keep television football tradition alive by hiring Madden and Summerall.

Of course, that is exactly what executives at FOX planned. By 1994, it had become impossible to separate the team of Madden and Summerall from professional football coverage on television. The two announcers signed contracts shortly afterward and began announcing for FOX on the very first weekend the network began its football coverage.

David Hill, president of FOX Sports, said there was never any question about hiring Madden in the broadcast booth. "He's the best sports communicator in the world — he can make an ordinary game sound great and a great game sound superlative," said Hill of Madden. "It's very simple for the viewers. They realize Madden and Summerall are the best."

The people who work with Madden say that over the years he has become a much better analyst and much better broadcaster. He has closely followed and mastered all the advances in television technology and kept up with every tiny change in the game. "He told me once that a good coach can never take it easy, can never slow down, that if a coach did that, he'd start to lose all the time. He has that same attitude in television. He will never slow down for fear that it will make him less effective as an analyst," said his director, Grossman.

Writers said that Madden was so famous that FOX needed him far more than he needed FOX. "Madden provided FOX with instant credibility and (with Summerall) an announcing team that had done more than 200 NFC games," wrote Lawrence Linderman in *TV Guide.*

John Madden's hair is white now. His ties still don't fit right under his shirt collar. His shirts are still too small for his bulging stomach, and his shoelaces are still untied. He's still making up crazy words to describe football, still challenging blimps to races, and still looking for odd players for the All-Madden team. There's no reason to think that he won't keep broadcasting football games well into the next century, when someone even faster than Barry Sanders and quicker than Emmitt Smith will be tackled hard, and Madden will yell into the microphone, "POW!"

STATISTICS

John Madden
coach, Oakland Raiders

Year	W-L-T	PCT	PTS	OPP	PR
1969	12-1-1	.893	377	242	1-1
1970	8-4-2	.643	300	293	1-1
1971	8-4-2	.643	344	278	
1972	10-3-1	.750	365	248	0-1
1973	9-4-1	.679	292	175	1-1
1974	12-2-0	.857	355	118	1-1
1975	11-3-0	.786	375	255	1-1
1976	13-1-0	.929	350	237	3-0
1977	11-3-0	.857	351	230	1-1
1978	9-7-0	.563	311	283	
TOTALS:	103-32-7	.750	3420	2359	9-7

W	win
L	loss
T	tie
PCT	percentage
PTS	points scored
OPP	points opponent scored
PR	playoff record

JOHN MADDEN
A CHRONOLOGY

1936   Born in Austin, Minnesota.

1959   After a successful college career, is drafted by the Philadelphia Eagles. A training-camp knee injury, however, prevents him from ever playing a game in the NFL.

1964   Coach Don Coryell names Madden to be his assistant at San Diego State University.

1967   Named linebackers coach by Oakland Raiders.

1969   Becomes head coach of the Oakland Raiders at age 33, the youngest coach in the NFL; leads team to a 12-1-1 record and AFL championship.

1972   Leads Raiders to a first-place finish in AFC West—the third time in four years he has done that, and the first of five consecutive first-place seasons.

1976   Leads Oakland Raiders to their most successful season, 13-1, which culminates in a victory in the Super Bowl over the Minnesota Vikings, 32-14.

1978   Retires as head coach with longest tenure and most victories of all Raider coaches.

1979   Joins CBS Sports as broadcaster, where he is paired with Pat Summerall.

1982   Wins first of nine Emmy awards.

1994   Joins FOX-TV.

SUGGESTIONS FOR FURTHER READING

Chadd, Norman. "Whack! Boom! Doink!, Sportscaster John Madden," *Sports Illustrated*, December 7, 1992.

King, Peter. "Busman's Holiday," *Sports Illustrated*, November 26, 1990.

Linderman, Lawrence. "Hail King John," *TV Guide*, September 3, 1994.

John Madden, with Dave Anderson. *Hey, Wait a Minute (I Wrote a Book)*. New York: Villard Books, 1984.

John Madden, with Dave Anderson. *One Knee Equals Two Feet (And Everything Else You Need To Know About Football)*. New York: Villard Books, 1986.

John Madden, with Dave Anderson. *One Size Doesn't Fit All*. New York: Villard Books, 1988.

McCollister, J. "Boom!: It's John Madden" *Saturday Evening Post*, January/February, 1988.

Moore, K. "Double Dip For Daly City," *Sports Illustrated*, October 16, 1987.

ABOUT THE AUTHOR

Bruce Chadwick, a longtime columnist with the New York Daily News, has written over 300 magazine articles, 13 nonfiction books, and one novel. Among his books are *When the Game was Black and White*, and *American Summers: Minor League Baseball*. He is the author of *Joe Namath* and *Deion Sanders* for Chelsea House's "Football Legends" series. Chadwick is an associate resident fellow at the Smithsonian where he lectures on baseball's role in American society.

INDEX